ASCOTT UNDER WYCHWOOD BURTON-ON-THE-WATER BURFOR
CHARLBURY CHIPPING NORTON CHURCHILL COLESBOURN
LOWER SLAUGHTER NORTHLEACH STOW-ON-THE WOL
CHELTENHAM BISHOPS CLEEVE BLOCKLEY BROADWAY CHARLTO
KINGS CHIPPING CAMPDEN CLEEVE HIL CRANHAM DURSLEY HAILE
PAINSWICK PRINKNASH ABBEY BISLEY STROUD ULEY WINCHCOME
WOODCHESTER BIBURY CHALFORD DUNTISBOURNE FAIRFOR
LECHLADE MINCHINAMPTON NAILSWORTH SOUTH CERNE
TETBURY ASCOTT UNDER WYCHWOOD BURTON-ON-THE-WATE
BURFORD CHARLBURY CHIPPING NORTON CHURCHIL
COLESBOURNE LOWER SLAUGHTER NORTHLEACH STOW-ON-TH
WOLD CHELTENHAM BISHOPS CLEEVE BLOCKLEY BROADWA
CHARLTON KINGS CHIPPING CAMPDEN CLEEVE HIL CRANHA
DURSLEY HAILES PAINSWICK PRINKNASH ABBEY BISLEY STROU
ULEY WINCHCOMBE WOODCHESTER BIBURY CHALFOR
DUNTISBOURNE FAIRFORD LECHLADE MINCHINAMPTO
NAILSWORTH SOUTH CERNEY TETBURY BISHOPS CLEEVE BLOCKLE
BROADWAY CHARLTON KINGS CHIPPING CAMPDEN CLEEVE H
CRANHAM DURSLEY HAILES PAINSWICK PRINKNASH ABBEYASCOT
UNDER WYCHWOOD BURTON-ON-THE-WATER BURFOR
CHARLBURY CHIPPING NORTON CHURCHILL COLESBOURN
LOWER SLAUGHTER NORTHLEACH STOW-ON-THE WOL
CHELTENHAM BISHOPS CLEEVE BLOCKLEY BROADWAY CHARLTO
KINGS CHIPPING CAMPDEN CLEEVE HIL CRANHAM DURSLEY HAILE
PAINSWICK PRINKNASH ABBEY BISLEY STROUD ULEY WINCHCOME
WOODCHESTER BIBURY CHALFORD DUNTISBOURNE FAIRFOR
LECHLADE MINCHINAMPTON NAILSWORTH SOUTH CERNE
TETBURY ASCOTT UNDER WYCHWOOD BURTON-ON-THE-WATE
BURFORD CHARLBURY CHIPPING NORTON CHURCHIL
COLESBOURNE LOWER SLAUGHTER NORTHLEACH STOW-ON-TH
WOLD CHELTENHAM BISHOPS CLEEVE BLOCKLEY BROADWA
CHARLTON KINGS CHIPPING CAMPDEN CLEEVE HIL CRANHA
DURSLEY HAILES PAINSWICK PRINKNASH ABBEY BISLEY STROU
ULEY WINCHCOMBE WOODCHESTER BIBURY CHALFOR
DUNTISBOURNE FAIRFORD LECHLADE MINCHINAMPTO
NAILSWORTH SOUTH CERNEY TETBURY BISHOPS CLEEVE BLOCKLE
BROADWAY CHARLTON KINGS CHIPPING CAMPDEN CLEEVE H
CRANHAM DURSLEY HAILES PAINSWICK PRINKNASH ABBEY HAILES

Francis Frith's

COTSWOLD
LIVING MEMORIES

Stroud, High Street c1960 S224062

photographs of the mid twentieth century

Francis Frith's

COTSWOLD
LIVING MEMORIES

Robert Cook & Andrew Shouler

First published in the United Kingdom in 2001 by
Frith Book Company Ltd

Hardback Edition 2001
ISBN 1-85937-255-4

Paperback Edition 2004
ISBN 1-85937-890-0

British Library Cataloguing in Publication Data

Francis Frith's Cotswold Living Memories
Robert Cook & Andrew Shouler

Frith Book Company Ltd
Frith's Barn, Teffont,
Salisbury, Wiltshire SP3 5QP
Tel: +44 (0) 1722 716 376
Email: info@francisfrith.co.uk
www.francisfrith.co.uk

Printed and bound in Great Britain

Front Cover: Stow-on-the-Wold, The Square c1950 S260024

The colour-tinting is for illustrative purposes only, and is not intended to be historically accurate

contents

Francis Frith: Victorian Pioneer

FRANCIS FRITH, Victorian founder of the world-famous photographic archive, was a complex and multi-talented man. A devout Quaker and a highly successful Victorian businessman, he was both philosophical by nature and pioneering in outlook.

By 1855 Francis Frith had already established a wholesale grocery business in Liverpool, and sold it for the astonishing sum of £200,000, which is the equivalent today of over £15,000,000. Now a very rich man, he was able to indulge his passion for travel. As a child he had pored over travel books written by early explorers, and his fancy and imagination had been stirred by family holidays to the sublime mountain regions of Wales and Scotland. 'What lands of spirit-stirring and enriching scenes and places!' he had written. He was to return to these scenes of grandeur in later years to 'recapture the thousands of vivid and tender memories', but with a different purpose. Now in his thirties, and captivated by the new science of photography, Frith set out on a series of pioneering journeys to the Nile regions that occupied him from 1856 until 1860.

Intrigue and Adventure

He took with him on his travels a specially-designed wicker carriage that acted as both dark-room and sleeping chamber. These far-flung journeys were packed with intrigue and adventure. In his life story, written when he was sixty-three, Frith tells of being held captive by bandits, and of fighting 'an awful midnight battle to the very point of surrender with a deadly pack of hungry, wild dogs'. Sporting flowing Arab costume, Frith arrived at Akaba by camel sixty years before Lawrence, where he encountered 'desert princes and rival sheikhs, blazing with jewel-hilted swords'.

During these extraordinary adventures he was assiduously exploring the desert regions bordering the Nile and patiently recording the antiquities and peoples with his camera. He was the first photographer to venture beyond the sixth cataract. Africa was still the mysterious 'Dark Continent', and Stanley and Livingstone's historic meeting was a decade into the future. The conditions for picture taking confound belief. He laboured for hours in his wicker dark-room in the sweltering heat of the desert, while the volatile chemicals fizzed dangerously in their trays. Often he was forced to work in remote tombs and caves where conditions

were cooler. Back in London he exhibited his photographs and was 'rapturously cheered' by members of the Royal Society. His reputation as a photographer was made overnight. An eminent modern historian has likened their impact on the population of the time to that on our own generation of the first photographs taken on the surface of the moon.

Venture of a Life-Time

Characteristically, Frith quickly spotted the opportunity to create a new business as a specialist publisher of photographs. He lived in an era of immense and sometimes violent change. For the poor in the early part of Victoria's reign work was a drudge and the hours long, and people had precious little free time to enjoy themselves. Most had no transport other than a cart or gig at their disposal, and had not travelled far beyond the

boundaries of their own town or village. However, by the 1870s, the railways had threaded their way across the country, and Bank Holidays and half-day Saturdays had been made obligatory by Act of Parliament. All of a sudden the ordinary working man and his family were able to enjoy days out and see a little more of the world.

With characteristic business acumen, Francis Frith foresaw that these new tourists would enjoy having souvenirs to commemorate their days out. In 1860 he married Mary Ann Rosling and set out with the intention of photographing every city, town and village in Britain. For the next thirty years he travelled the country by train and by pony and trap, producing fine photographs of seaside resorts and beauty spots that were keenly bought by millions of Victorians. These prints were painstakingly pasted into family albums and pored over during the dark nights of winter, rekindling precious memories of summer excursions.

The Rise of Frith & Co

Frith's studio was soon supplying retail shops all over the country. To meet the demand he gathered about him a small team of photographers, and published the work of independent artist-photographers of the calibre of Roger Fenton and Francis Bedford. In order to gain some understanding of the scale of Frith's business one only has to look at the catalogue issued by Frith & Co in 1886: it runs to some 670 pages, listing not only many thousands of views of the British Isles but also many photographs of most European countries,

and China, Japan, the USA and Canada – note the sample page shown above from the hand-written *Frith & Co* ledgers detailing pictures taken. By 1890 Frith had created the greatest specialist photographic publishing company in the world, with over 2,000 outlets – more than the combined number that Boots and W H Smith have today! The picture on the right shows the *Frith & Co* display board at Ingleton in the Yorkshire Dales (left of window). Beautifully constructed with a mahogany frame and gilt inserts, it could display up to a dozen local scenes.

Postcard Bonanza

The ever-popular holiday postcard we know today took many years to develop. In 1870 the Post Office issued the first plain cards, with a pre-printed stamp on one face. In 1894 they allowed other publishers' cards to be sent through the mail with an attached adhesive halfpenny stamp. Demand grew rapidly, and in 1895 a new size of postcard was permitted called the court card, but there was little room for illustration. In 1899, a year after Frith's death, a new card measuring 5.5 x 3.5 inches became the standard format, but it was not until 1902 that the divided back came into being, with address and message on one face and a full-size illustration on the other. *Frith & Co* were in the vanguard of postcard development, and Frith's sons Eustace and Cyril continued their father's monumental task, expanding the number of views offered to the public and recording more and more places in Britain, as the coasts and countryside were opened up to mass travel.

Francis Frith died in 1898 at his villa in Cannes, his great project still growing. The archive he created continued in business for another seventy years. By 1970 it contained over a third of a million pictures of 7,000 cities, towns and villages. The massive photographic record Frith has left to us stands as a living monument to a special and very remarkable man.

Frith's Archive: A Unique Legacy

FRANCIS FRITH'S legacy to us today is of immense significance and value, for the magnificent archive of evocative photographs he created provides a unique record of change in 7,000 cities, towns and villages throughout Britain over a century and more. Frith and his fellow studio photographers revisited locations many times down the years to update their views, compiling for us an enthralling and colourful pageant of British life and character.

We tend to think of Frith's sepia views of Britain as nostalgic, for most of us use them to conjure up memories of places in our own lives with which we have family associations. It often makes us forget that to Francis Frith they were records of daily life as it was actually being lived in the cities, towns and villages of his day. The Victorian age was one of great and often bewildering change for ordinary people, and though the pictures evoke an impression of slower times, life was as busy and hectic as it is today.

We are fortunate that Frith was a photographer of the people, dedicated to recording the minutiae of everyday life. For it is this sheer wealth of visual data, the painstaking chronicle of changes in dress, transport, street layouts, buildings, housing, engineering and landscape that captivates us so much today. His remarkable images offer us a powerful link with the past and with the lives of our ancestors.

Today's Technology

Computers have now made it possible for Frith's many thousands of images to be accessed almost instantly. In the Frith archive today, each photograph is carefully 'digitised' then stored on a CD Rom. Frith archivists can locate a single photograph amongst thousands within seconds. Views can be catalogued and sorted under a variety of categories of place and content to the immediate benefit of researchers.

Inexpensive reference prints can be created for them at the touch of a mouse button, and a wide range of books and other printed materials assembled and published for a wider, more general readership. The day-to-day workings of the archive are very different from how they were in Francis Frith's time: imagine the herculean task of sorting through eleven tons of glass negatives as Frith had to do to locate a particular sequence of pictures! Yet the archive still prides itself on maintaining the same high

THE FRANCIS FRITH COLLECTION

Photographic publishers since 1860

HOME | PHOTO SEARCH | BOOKS | PORTFOLIO | GALLERY   MY CART

Products | History | Other Collections | Contact us | Help?

your town,
your village

365,000 photographs of 7,000 towns and villages, taken between 1860 & 1970.

The Frith Archive

The Frith Archive is the remarkable legacy of its energetic and visionary founder. Today, the Frith archive is the only nationally important archive of its kind still in private ownership.

The Collection is world-renowned for the extraordinary quality of its images.

The Gallery

This month The Frith Gallery features images from "Frith's Egypt".

the **FRITH**gallery

News...

Image update complete. An additional 5,000 images have been added and the quality of all images has now been improved.

Sample Chapters available. The first selection of sample chapters from the Frith Book Co.'s extensive range is now available. All are offered in Pdf format for easy downloading and viewing.

explore FRITH

Search thousands of photographs from one of the worlds' great archives.

Town search

GO

County search

Select a county

GO

See Frith at www.francisfrith.co.uk

standards of excellence laid down by Francis Frith, including the painstaking cataloguing and indexing of every view.

It is curious to reflect on how the internet now allows researchers in America and elsewhere greater instant access to the archive than Frith himself ever enjoyed. Many thousands of individual views can be called up on screen within seconds on one of the Frith internet sites, enabling people living continents away to revisit the streets of their ancestral home town, or view places in Britain where they have enjoyed holidays. Many overseas researchers welcome the chance to view special theme selections, such as transport, sports, costume and ancient monuments.

We are certain that Francis Frith would have heartily approved of these modern developments in imaging techniques, for he himself was always working at the very limits of Victorian photographic technology.

The Value of the Archive Today

Because of the benefits brought by the computer, Frith's images are increasingly studied by social historians, by researchers into genealogy and ancestory, by architects, town planners, and by teachers and schoolchildren involved in local history projects.

In addition, the archive offers every one of us an opportunity to examine the places where we and our families have lived and worked down the years. Highly successful in Frith's own era, the archive is now, a century and more on, entering a new phase of popularity.

The Past in Tune with the Future

Historians consider the Francis Frith Collection to be of prime national importance. It is the only archive of its kind remaining in private ownership and has been valued at a million pounds. However, this figure is now rapidly increasing as digital technology enables more and more people around the world to enjoy its benefits.

Francis Frith's archive is now housed in an historic timber barn in the beautiful village of Teffont in Wiltshire. Its founder would not recognize the archive office as it is today. In place of the many thousands of dusty boxes containing glass plate negatives and an all-pervading odour of photographic chemicals, there are now ranks of computer screens. He would be amazed to watch his images travelling round the world at unimaginable speeds through network and internet lines.

The archive's future is both bright and exciting. Francis Frith, with his unshakeable belief in making photographs available to the greatest number of people, would undoubtedly approve of what is being done today with his lifetime's work. His photographs, depicting our shared past, are now bringing pleasure and enlightenment to millions around the world a century and more after his death.

Cotswold Living Memories
An Introduction

The Cotswolds are an upland area of limestone. The escarpment ('the Cotswold edge') rises above the broad valley of the River Severn, and the land slopes gently away eastward. The main area of the Cotswolds is contained in modern Gloucestershire, but it extends eastwards into Oxfordshire and to a degree north into Warwickshire and south into Wiltshire. To preserve its identity, the area has been proclaimed an area of outstanding natural beauty.

The limestone is called oolite (meaning egg stone, because its constituent granules are likened to fish roe), which makes an excellent building material. It varies in shade from a warm honey colour in the north to a colder grey in the south. Many rivers and streams rise in the wolds; the majority flow south-eastwards to join the River Thames, while a few flow west into the Severn Vale. The water is crystal-clear after its passage through the limestone; this clarity was used to advantage in the various processes of the wool industry in medieval and later times. However, even in this relatively small area of some 40 miles by 25 miles there is divergence in the character of the landscape. The northern area has the undulating wolds, whilst in the south, particularly in the area around Stroud, the valleys are deep and steep-sided, with the rivers and streams at their base providing water

power. The area is believed to have been originally forested, a link with the great Oxfordshire and Northamptonshire forests to the east and the Forest of Dean to the west across the Severn. Although limestone is much stronger than chalk, it is no less soluble. It is surprising, perhaps, that there are no caves, but groundwater drains freely down through the porous rock without having to carve a passage. If it was not for shale and thick alluvium on the surface, the Cotswolds would be as dry and streamless as the Chilterns, and we would be looking at a very different landscape.

The earliest inhabitants were Neolithic people, groups of Stone Age farmers who migrated north from the chalk downlands of Wiltshire and Dorset. Their burial chambers, long barrows, have been found in various locations and excavated. The Iron Age peoples from Europe reached the area in about 500 BC. Their hill forts remain to this day in considerable numbers, some with quite elaborate systems of defensive earthworks. After their invasion in AD 43, The Roman army moved quickly north and west, eventually driving native Britons into Wales and the north-west. The Cotswolds were important to the Romans: the area formed a convenient buffer zone between the quickly-subdued south and east and the problematic north and west. The Fosse Way, running south-west to north-east, became a suitable road for troop movement and, together with Ermine and Akeman Streets, for trade generally. These roads all met at Cirencester (the Roman Corinium), which developed into a commercial centre second only to London in importance. The Saxons invaded from the east following the departure of the Romans. Although they left few physical remains apart from one or two churches, their presence lives on in place names. Indeed, some say the name Cotswolds derives from the Saxon word 'cot', meaning animal enclosure.

However, it was the Normans who introduced sheep - the animals which brought wealth to the area. A particular breed, known for a thick long fleece, was called Cotswold Lion. Incidentally, when the wool trade declined, so did the breed; it was only saved from extinction by the setting up of the Cotswold Sheep Society about 100 years ago. It is believed that over 500,000 sheep were kept in the Cotswolds at the zenith of the wool trade, which engaged more than fifty per cent of the population. As many as 20,000 animals would pass through the important sheep fairs of the northern Cotswold towns such as Stow on the Wold. The wool was originally exported to Europe; the merchants who organised the trade earned themselves a fortune. The merchants then brought weavers from Europe to teach the local population the art of cloth production, and became even

richer! The wool and cloth industry dominated the country's economy for several centuries during the Middle Ages, and it is worth remembering that the Lord Chancellor still sits on a woolsack in the chamber of the House of Lords.

With their considerable wealth, the merchants became local benefactors, building large, beautiful houses and churches. The churches were built, perhaps, to salve their consciences and to provide a pathway to heaven. The merchants undoubtedly prospered at the expense of the poor spinners and weavers, who depended upon them for wool supplies. The spinners and weavers also depended on the fulling mills, where the woven material was taken for shrinking and cloth finishing. Fullers earth, so necessary in broadcloth preparation, was found near Stroud, and this area became important with workers migrating to the valleys around.

With the country's rising population, mass production methods were required to clothe the people. This required heavy-duty machinery and the continuous power of steam, which in turn required coal - a commodity not found on the Cotswolds. However, coal could be found in the north of the country, and Yorkshire became the centre of woollen cloth manufacture. The exception was around Stroud and its valleys: the Stroudwater canal was opened in 1779 to bring coal from the Forest of Dean and the Midlands. Unfortunately, 13 locks were needed to accommodate the change of levels over the 8 miles from Stroud down to the River Severn. Even with the later help of the railway, Stroud could not compete with Yorkshire in quantity of output, although several mills survived producing fine-quality cloth.

However, the Cotswold area generally suffered decline in trade from the 1650s. Various schemes were tried to maintain or stimulate growth. Perhaps the most bizarre was the Act of Burial in Wool: this required all burial shrouds to be made from wool rather than linen. Such schemes were unsuccessful. With no alternative work, and with starvation setting in, the population moved away to find other livelihoods, leaving just a few farmers and their labourers. The villages and towns thus remained in their unspoiled state, which makes them so attractive to the tourists of the 20th and 21st centuries. There are few areas left in the country where the architecture and layout of medieval, 16th-, 17th- and 18th-century buildings and the correlated lives of their occupants have been so well preserved. This fact was recognised by Friths when these photographs were taken some 50 and 60 years ago. We, the authors, are enthusiasts for architectural and topographical history, and we are delighted that these Frith photographs reveal this history so clearly.

Our approach to the area is to divide it into five regions:

1) The northern and eastern Cotswolds, including Oxfordshire. This is an area of undulating wolds interspersed with wide valleys containing rivers and streams. The buildings, which include magnificent wool churches, date back to the medieval days of sheep and wool, and are constructed in warm honey-coloured stone.

2) The western escarpment, rising up to over 1000 feet from the Severn Vale in the north and the Vale of Berkeley in the south, dominates all views in the area. At its highest in the north, with a summit of 1083 feet at Cleeve Hill near Winchcombe, it is still some 800 feet high farther south; it is well-wooded throughout its 40 miles' length.

3) Cheltenham lies within the western escarpment, but it deserves attention in its own right. Nestled in the Cotswolds, it earned fame as a spa town. Its tree-lined streets, parks, grand Georgian houses and a modern shopping centre all make it quite exceptional. St Mary's Church, standing above all the daily hurly-burly in the heart of town, was originally Norman, with later additions. Finely-traceried windows, including a rose window 45 feet round, are truly magnificent. But perhaps Cheltenham is most famous for its distinguished Ladies College and its horse racing.

4) The south Cotswolds is an area undulating in the east, with valleys becoming steeper and deeper to the west, again with swift-flowing streams. The stone here is a cool silvery grey, and the buildings are still magnificent.

5) Cirencester lies in the region of the south Cotswolds, but it deserves special attention as a significant Roman settlement and because of its historic importance from being placed at a junction of ancient roads. For many years a market and hunting centre, it has many impressive old buildings, including the remains of an abbey. The magnificent, mainly Perpendicular church has a unique three-storey porch built in the 16th century by the local guilds, and there is some fine screen work. Henry I's St John's Hospital has been restored, and there is a museum with Roman antiquities. A park of 3000 acres surrounds an 18th-century house which was once associated with Alexander Pope. There are over 2000 years of history to enjoy here.

The North-Eastern Cotswolds

Ascott under Wychwood, London Lane c1950
A140002
Ascott is situated on the River Evenlode in Oxfordshire, just east of the main A361 Burford to Chipping Norton road. The torch symbol on the early cast iron school sign indicates the torch of knowledge; it was superseded by a sign showing a traditional uniformed schoolboy and girl. The village stands by the Oxford to Worcester railway line, and has a functional station served by a few local Thames trains. Wychwood Forest covered 150 square miles in the Middle Ages, but is now reduced to around 1500 acres.

▼ Ascott Under Wychwood c1950 A140008
This peaceful scene shows neat dry stone walls and elms flourishing - in the early 1970s, Dutch elm disease ravaged so many. The Swan pub looks cosy, and would have welcomed many a weary labourer after the day's toil. The local Oxford brew from Morrell's could not be bettered.

▼ Ascott Under Wychwood, Langley Mill c1950 A140011
The mill was driven by the River Evenlode. It was still working at the time of this photograph - note the sack lying over the half stable door and the full sack by the door. The well-cared-for, neat-and-tidy appearance is commendable.

▲ Bourton-on-the-Water The Bridges c1955
B392037
The town is now an unashamed tourist centre. This view shows the fine footbridges over the River Windrush, some dating from before Roman times. The Fosse Way made the boundary between the military zone to the north and the civil zone to the south, and it crossed the Windrush at a ford by Bourton Bridge. The road was built by the 2nd Legion, and this was commemorated by a stone plaque on the bridge.

◄ **Bourton-on-the-Water The Green c1955** B392040 This view of the low footbridges is taken further along from No B392037: the rusticated bridge (dating from 1756) in the foreground can be seen in the background of that photograph. From Norman times the town prospered with the wool trade, and suffered when this declined. Fortunately, it revived through tourism.

◄ **Bourton-on- the-Water The Village c1955** B392077
This north-east view of the High Street is devoid of all the street furniture and clutter deemed so necessary today. The church of St Lawrence, originally dating from Norman times, was rebuilt in 1784, except for the chancel. Note the lead-covered dome and the lozenge-shaped clock face. The plain building next to the church is the former rectory; it dates from the 1820s. The substantial building housing Ball's stores has a date stone of 1902 on the pediment, and looks the epitome of Edwardian optimism.

◄ Bourton-on the-Water Entrance to the Studio Cafe c1950 B392058
After taking refreshment at the cafe, these visitors look set to browse amongst the antiques. Note the dressed stone window heads and mullions on the ground and first floor.

▼ Bourton-on-the Water c1960 B392586
This view was taken from a little south of No B392077, and shows a delightful 17th-century house with ornate window heads right of centre. There are not too many cars to spoil the scene just yet, but a Ford Popular parked in front of the shops betokens a modern age.

◄ Burford, High Street c1960
B369024
We are at an excellent spot to sit and watch the steady but not overwhelming flow of traffic trundling up the long street; we are looking toward the west side of the High Street. The trees are in leaf, and the summer sun casts shadows. There are many little corners to explore and enjoy in this town, which is rich in wool cloth, leather and paper-making traditions. The ridge on the skyline separates the Windrush Valley from that of the Evenlode some 5 miles north.

Francis Frith's Cotswold Living Memories

▼ **Burford, High Street c1960** B369023

This view is taken from the opposite side of the road and gives us a better view of Swan Florists and the ridge. Just left of the pollarded lime tree we can glimpse the proud spire of St John the Baptist church, which stands by the winding river. It dates from Norman times, and wealth from the wool trade financed its enlargement to something approaching a small cathedral. In May 1649, some 340 mutinous troops from the New Model Army were herded into this building as prisoners. After several days, three ringleaders were taken outside and shot, and the remainder were dismissed from the regiment. The War Memorial in the foreground epitomises the sacrifices of all services in two World Wars.

▼ **Burford, High Street c1960** B369017

We are looking north, downhill towards the three-arched bridge over the rippling River Windrush, which is just beyond among the willows. The Priory, with its three gables, an Elizabethan mansion rebuilt in 1808 at half the original size, was home to William Lenthall. He was speaker of the Long Parliament. Buying the house in 1634, he retired here after the Restoration. The Highway Hotel dates from about 1500. Charles I is said to have slept the night at a local inn.

▲ **Burford, Sheep Street c1950** B369008

A pub called the Lamb and the Bay Tree Hotel - what more could such a beautiful street in this medieval town need to claim perfection? The hotel dates from the 1650s. Sheep Street was the original London road before a new road (the present A40 trunk road) was built to the south in 1812.

◀ **Charlbury, Church Street c1950** C444003
Situated on the eastern wolds of Oxfordshire, this is an attractive little stone town, looking from its hillside over the River Evenlode, and the remnant of Wychwood Forest. The broad sweep of Church Street ends at the entrance to the graveyard with its low stone wall. The Bell Inn on the left dates from around 1700. Nearby is Cornbury, a 600-acre deer park and a Tudor, 17th- and 18th-century mansion, once home to Elizabeth I's advisor and lover Robert Dudley, Earl of Leicester.

▼ **Charlbury, Church Street c1950** C444007
This is a charming scene: mum and baby, representing the future, walk by cars that would now be collectors' items on the right of the street. The old boy looks out from his porch back along the street in the direction of Sheep Street, where Hunt, Edmunds & Co are advertising ales, wines and spirits. Perhaps he is off for a quick one!

▼ **Charlbury, Sheep Street c1950** C444008
Here is a closer view of Hunt & Edmunds' alcoholic haven. It may be early morning, with the schoolgirl off to lessons; or maybe it is the weekend, and she is heading for that curious little shop which combines fish and fruit among its wares. Mr Brooks has a substantial corner shop on the opposite side; the date stone records 1890 as the commencing date for his trade as an ironmonger and hot and cold water fitter. Not many had hot water in those good old days!

▲ **Charlbury, The View from Grammar School Hill c1950** C444006
This lovely scene shows the 14th-century church tower of St Mary's rising high on the horizon. Note the building work at the bottom of the slope: the scaffolding uses timber poles instead of modern alloys, and the lack of guard rails would give the modern safety officer a headache! The town's prosperity, like its more western counterparts, was based upon sheep, but in the 19th century glove-making became dominant, employing 1000 people at one time.

◄ **Chipping Norton The Leys c1945**
C288002
This is the highest town in Oxfordshire; a fine avenue of trees here along The Leys leads up to the ridge. This is a distinguished market town, situated facing west. Numerous inns, still extant, testify to its thriving on an old coach road (now the A44) from Worcester and onwards to Oxford and London.

▼ **Chipping Norton, View of the Cotswolds c1960** C288067
This is an evocative view across the eastern wolds in midsummer, with oats ripening in the foreground. The hills above the western escarpment form the skyline.

▼ **Chipping Norton, The Rollright Stones c1960** C288073
Just north of Chipping Norton, in the parish of Great Rollright, lie the Rollright Stones, set in a circle about 100 feet in diameter. Some of the original eleven stones have been broken up and the pieces laid around. It dates back some 3,500 years to the Bronze Age, and was a ritual stone circle and burial chamber. The Tudor historian and traveller, John Camden, records a legend that the stones were the knights and soldiers of an army turned to stone by a local witch.

▲ **Chipping Norton Market Street c1945**
C288029
What a pity that F Sole went in for being a family butcher when the name would have better suited a fishmonger! The Ford 8 van parked opposite this shop has white-painted mudguards; this testifies to a wartime need for it to be seen by fellow motorists and pedestrians during the blackout.

◀ **Chipping Norton High Street c1945** C288026
The Town Hall, on the left, dates from 1842; its imposing stone portico faces onto the High Street rather than the Market Square - which, as has become common in the modern age, is being used as a car park. The Co-operative Society frontage makes a fine contribution to the majestic terrace on the right. Portraits inside the Town Hall include that of Alderman Wilkins. He was the only English mayor in Queen Victoria's jubilee year who had been mayor when she acceded to the throne.

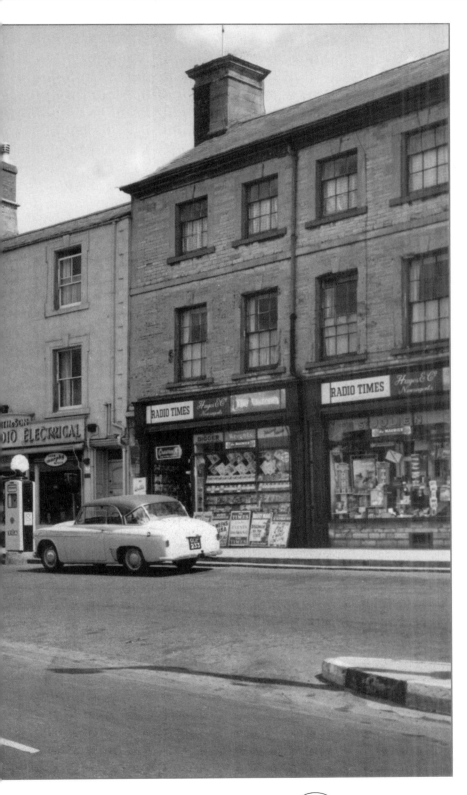

**Chipping Norton
High Street c1960**
C288063
The central archway
of the Crown &
Cushion Hotel indicates
that it was a coaching
inn with two coaches
driving into the
courtyard daily to pick
up and set down
passengers, and
perhaps to allow them
time for a meal and
change of horses.

◄ **Churchill**
The Memorial c1960
C290005
The village of Churchill lies about three miles south of Chipping Norton. This small place was the birthplace of William Smith (who died in 1839). This gentleman produced the first geological map of England, and is known as 'the father of English geology'.

◄ **Chipping Norton, High Street c1959** C288053
The High Street broadens into the Market Square, where a market was held every Wednesday. The National Provincial Bank reminds us that this was indeed a provincial age, a long time away from the insipid uniformity of our so-called multi-cultural society, which does its homogenising work through the mass media. We can also see that some forty years ago motorists parked sensibly and without the need for modern regimentation.

▼ **Colesbourne, Lower Hilcot c1960** C453010
About midway between Cheltenham and Cirencester, in the valley of the River Churn, lies the village of Colesbourne. Here an inviting gateway leads to the hamlet of Lower Hilcot.

◄ **Colesbourne, Lower Hilcot c1960** C453012
This view shows the ford across the Churn. The collapsed handrail makes the planked footbridge look precarious. The abandoned cart wheel, by the edge of the weir, would have done some trundling around the busy streets, fields and farm ways before giving way to an age that no longer needed it. The vernacular Cotswold architecture of the 18th-century dwellings makes an attractive backdrop. Note the substantial drip courses to the gable chimneys. The whole view might have been painted by John Constable.

◀ **Lower Slaughter
The Mill and Pond c1950**
L313008
A water mill has stood here since Norman times, but this red brick corn mill dates from the early 1800s. The water wheel appears to be in good order, and the fine brick stack displays stone drip courses. Keeping the water off the stonework has been of much concern to local architects in this damp environment. The long, low 17th-century house, right, has fine stone-mullioned and drip-headed windows. The sign on the dry stone wall reads 'cycles for hire', which would be the perfect transport for a place like this.

◄ Lower Slaughter
The Village c1950 L313001
Lower Slaughter typifies the traditional Cotswolds appearance: even the council houses have stone-slated roofs. Here we see an attractive group of cottages beside the stone-faced bank of the Slaughter Brook. The Gothic-style structure in the centre covers a well, so important before the days of piped water and water works.

▼ Lower Slaughter
The Bridge c1950 L313005
Bridging the River Eye (which joins the Windrush just south of Bourton-on-the-Water), these little low bridges of ancient weathered stone have attracted artists to the area for years. The placename is misleading: there is so much beauty here, including an old dovecote in the manor garden and a rebuilt church which retains a late 12th-century nave arcade.

◄ Northleach, Market Square
c1950 N125001
This little town, not much more than a village since it lost the wool trade, is situated on the central wolds between Cheltenham and Burford. Its past fame as a wool market reached western Europe, to which it exported cloth in the 15th century. The market place is east of the church; it is surrounded by fine houses dating from as early as the 1500s. The single-deck Bristol bus denotes the modern age as it pauses before proceeding east to Oxford, operating service 171 from Cheltenham. The journey took 2 ¼ hours, and ran five times a day - how amazing that seems to us now.

◄ **Northleach, The Green c1950**
N125032

This view looks in the opposite direction to No N125008. The supporting bearers to the timber frame of the Tudor building are visible in detail. The Ford Thames van bears a DD Gloucestershire registration; behind it we can just see the back of the latest Thames van which superseded it. The 15th-century tower of St Peter and St Paul church is on the skyline. It was built by the town's rich inhabitants during a period of religious fervour. This accounts for its striking majesty, with its mountains of masonry and panelled battlements; it rises to a stately 100 feet, so it is no wonder we can see it from here - it was meant to be seen for miles.

◀ Northleach, The Green c1950
N125008

The Green continues south from the market place. The half-timbered house on the right dates from Tudor times. Note how the timber work on the first floor projects, or jetties, from the ground floor stonework. It is interesting that the little cars and vans looked so much more friendly in these times: they are not ostentatious, and they leave room for these pedestrians and cyclists to roam carelessly about.

▼ Northleach, High Street c1965 N125054

The High Street runs along the east side of the market place. Here we see yet another half-timbered inn, the Red Lion, bearing testimony to the importance of the town in medieval and coaching days. A neat public toilet block is on the left, built in a Cotswold cottage style to harmonise with the street scene.

◀ Northleach, Market Square c1950 N125009

The half-timbered Kings Head inn in the background recalls the coaching age: Northleach was on the main London, Oxford, Gloucester and South Wales road (the main A40 road now by-passes the town). The square here is still a place for coaches, as we can see from the flourishing lines of the coach to the far right of the picture. The timber stocks supply another glimpse of historic ways: miscreants were bundled into the pillory to receive their punishment and supply enjoyment to the locals, who would be throwing rotten fruit, vegetables and eggs.

▼ **Northleach, Market Place c1965** N125056

This is the west side of the market place; we have a better view of the church with its massive tower and noble parapets. We can see the magnificent east window of the chancel and the unusual east window of the nave, both almost filling the wall with glass. There is also a selection of early 1960s motor cars to be seen; the large American Ford Estate car contrasts with its General Motors Vauxhall Victor neighbour. The Post Office building dates from the 16th century.

▼ **Northleach, Hampnett c1965** N125027

Hampnett is a small village a mile or so to the west of Northleach. Here we can see some contrasting architecture. On the right, the 18th-century dwellings have stone-slated roofs, gables and stone-mullioned windows. On the left, the later Victorian row, although still stone-built, has standard roof tiles. We can see a lady waiting by her front door for the roundsman who is approaching in his little Morris J-Type milk float. Roundsmen - butcher, baker, and fruiterer - were once the life-blood of isolated villages. A roofless barn is visible on the right, and the pony in the foreground appears to be posing for the photographer who has dared to enter the paddock.

▲ **Stow-on-the-Wold The Square c1950** S26002

This place was once a bustling wool centre, but it has not grown much since. When Daniel Defoe visited there were 20,000 sheep being sold here. This view shows the west end of the Market Square. Several routes enter town, but non disturb this pretty square. A couple, probably visitors admire the old market cros The pinnacled 15th-centur tower of St Edward's peeps up over the roof tops. The church was restored in the 1680s after being used to house prisoners during the Civil War; it was declared ruinous in 1657.

◀ **Stow-on-the-Wold The Square 1957**
S260045
Here is another view of the west end. The building with the projecting roof parapet on the left is the Talbot; one hundred years ago it was the largest hotel in town. It was established in 1714.

Stow-on-the-Wold The Square c1955

S260033

Looking northwards, we can see a good selection of 18th-century architecture; perhaps the most attractive is St Edward's House (next to the three-storey hotel) with Corinthian-topped fluted pilasters. A fine selection of cars show the predominance of modern compact styling and the demise of running boards. Four clergymen are disembarking from the sensible little Standard Eight.

▼ **Stow-on-the-Wold, The Square c1960** S260053

This view is dominated by the Victorian St Edward's Hall, perhaps the most famous house here. Unfortunately, we cannot see the handsome front doorway under a niche, which rises to a fine cornice and two fluted pilasters. The old stocks, sheltered by the trees, might well look quaint, but were once a place of ritual humiliation. They seem to have lost their seat, unless occupants were expected to sit on the grass.

▼ **Stow-on-the-Wold, The Square and St Edward's Hall c1950** S260014

Two little boys pose for posterity. There is enough traffic to decorate the scene, including the back end of a Hillman Minx in front of the Electricity Service Centre.

▲ **Stow-on-the-Wold The Square c1945**

S260015

This view reveals the very irregular shape of the square, which was said to be for the sake of protecting the traders and animals from inclement weather. An old rhyme says: 'Stow-on- the-Wold where the wind blows cold'. The Market Cross in the centre was erected in 1878. The panel shows the abbot of Evesham receiving the Charter for a weekly market from Henry I. There are glimpses of the church and St Edward's Hall - they act almost as end pieces to this rustic stage, where the traders include Deborah's Kitchen and H J Leftwich.

**Stow-on-the-Wold
The Post Office
c1955** S260043
The Post Office stands on the corner. The cast iron wall plaque prohibiting access for locomotives and heavy motor cars is more conspicuous than the 'No Waiting' sign: there was so little traffic to wait, and no need for double yellow lines and all the other traffic-oriented street clutter forty five years ago. But times would soon change.

Cheltenham

Cheltenham, The Promenade c1945 C75020
As we can see from all the parked cars, petrol is flowing again after wartime rationing. Cheltenham is (rather self consciously) the capital of the Cotswolds; it stands in the Vale under the western escarpment. In medieval times it was a small town, having been granted a charter in 1226. In 1716 a local hosier noted birds pecking at crystals in a field he owned; when he had the crystals analysed, they revealed a high mineral content. His daughter and son-in-law developed the site into a spa. Avenues of trees were planted, and buildings were erected. It became a popular watering place, where one drank the waters - unlike Bath, where one bathed. High society joined the throng, culminating in the visit by King George III and Queen Charlotte in 1788. The Duke of Wellington came to partake, and recommended the water to his officers. Cheltenham's future was assured. Building work proceeded apace, creating the well-planned town with fine Regency architecture which still remains today. The Promenade, with its central well-cared-for flower beds, and memorials to all those lives wasted in wars, is claimed as one of the most beautiful streets in England.

Cheltenham
Town Centre c1950 C75064
Although the passers-by are clearly displaying
late 1940s fashions here, this High Street view
still exudes the atmosphere of the 1930s.

Cheltenham, The Promenade Fountain c1945 C75025
Here we see the famous Neptune fountain (some say it is based upon the Trevi fountain in Rome), with Council Offices in the background and a glimpse of the Regency terraces to the left. People relax in the warm spring sunshine after the trauma of the recent war years.

Cheltenham, Montpelier Gardens c1950 C75072
The gardens are on the right of the picture; together with the Imperial Gardens, they testify to Cheltenham's love of flowers. The rotunda (now occupied by a bank) can be seen on the left. It was built in 1826, and was a concert hall and ballroom. Indeed, some of Gustav Holst's music received its first performance at the Rotunda; the famous composer was born in Cheltenham. The architectural link with Rome is maintained, as the Rotunda is reputedly based upon the Pantheon.

Cheltenham, Sandford Park, the Children's Pool c1950 C75078
It is a warm day, and children enjoy the delights of the large swimming pool. Sandford Park is just south of the town centre, and is skirted by the River Chelt on its eastern boundary.

Cheltenham, The Queen's Hotel c1955 C75091
This hotel was built on the site of the Imperial Well, and its attractive classical portico faces onto Imperial Gardens. It was built in the late 1830s; it is said that it was to have been called the King's Hotel, but King William IV died before it was complete. The Queen in its name obviously refers to Queen Victoria.

Cheltenham
The Centre c1960 C75129
In this view, the Regency splendour is all around. Over 40 years ago, the big multiple names, like John Collier, Stead and Stimpson and Lilley & Skinner, are all to be seen; they have yet to leave the main streets for the undercover shopping centre.

Cheltenham, The Devil's Chimney c1960 C75112
The stone which was used to build Cheltenham was quarried high up on the escarpment of Leckhamstead, some two or three miles away. The quarrymen left this column of stone, perhaps as a memorial to their efforts here; it is a famous landmark. It is known as the Devil's Chimney because locals say that it rises straight up from hell and that the devil is trapped inside.

Cheltenham, St Paul's College c1960 C75135
Cheltenham College was founded in 1841 as a public school for boys, and its buildings were designed in a Gothic style. In this view the trim, well-kept environment is echoed in the gleaming and solid-looking black Morris Oxford car. Cheltenham Ladies' College was founded in 1853 as a similar establishment for the fairer sex.

The Western Escarpment

Bishops Cleeve
The Village c1960 B531004
This Gloucestershire village lies below the fine slope of
Cleeve Hill in the Severn Valley on the A435 Cheltenham-
Evesham road. The tower of St Michael and All Angels can
be glimpsed over the thatched roof. The high escarpment
rises beyond. The village is some 150 feet above sea level,
700 feet below the summit of the hill.

▼ **Bishops Cleeve, Priory Lane c1960** B531006
Here the influence of the Vale is apparent from the fruit orchard, left, which is showing the effects of the prevailing south-westerlies which blow up the valley to create these pleasing leaning trees. The timber-framed thatched cottage may look less characteristic, but it is built from local materials.

▼ **Bishops Cleeve, from Cleeve Hill c1960** B531024
At nearly 1110 feet above sea level, the hill offers magnificent views across the Vale. It is the site of a hill fort, which probably dates from the Iron Age. From here we can see the tower of Bishop Cleeve church, highlighted by a patch of sunlight. Beyond the church tower and the strip of woodland flows the River Severn, and beyond that we can see the gaunt whale-back outline of the Malvern Hills.

▲ **Blockley, High Street c1950** B528005
Note the fine bow-fronted shop window, the semi-circular pediment above the door, and the stone-mullioned windows in the ancient property, right. Blockley stands high on the northern wolds above Broadway, and although it is situated in the sheep-rearing northern pastures, the village has an industrial past. In the early 1800s no less than six mills produced silk thread for the ribbon makers of Coventry. In this photograph, it is summertime: trees abound with leaves, while the sun casts its shadow across the tiny Esso petrol station.

◄ **Blockley**
The Church c1955
B528011
The tower of St Peter and St Paul was rebuilt in 1725 in ashlar masonry, but the main fabric of the building dates from Norman times, with additions built in the 14th century. The Bishops of Worcester had a palace close to where the manor house stands. Blockley was transferred from Worcestershire into Gloucestershire in 1931.

◀ **Broadway, The Green c195[...]**
B222055
Franklin's Stores looks busy -
shaded from the bright suns[...]
There is a little shade under [...]
tree for those with time to
contemplate life's (then) gen[...]
flow. The wide High Street g[...]
Broadway its name; the road
was built to cover two strea[...]
that flow either side of the o[...]
road. A coach is entering the
scene from the right, remind[...]
us that Broadway was on the
Worcester - London coachin[...]
route. The village leads away
from the Green towards the
western escarpment visible o[...]
the skyline.

Broadway, High Street c1960 B222078

There are lots of picturesque corners and old buildings, including the 17th-century Tudor house, St Eadburgh's church and the Lygon Arms, in this old Worcestershire village. It is no wonder, then, that artists like this one here are drawn to reproduce its essence on canvas. Fish Hill, 1,024 feet high, with an 18th-century tower at the summit, rises above the village.

Broadway, The Green c1955 B222057

We can almost feel the heat of this sunny day. Horse-drawn wagons were still not unusual in the 1950s English countryside, as we see here. During coaching days, inns abounded; among them was the curious little Fish Inn. The Cross Hands signpost nearby was placed on the site of a former gibbet where 3 innocent persons were hanged in 1661.

Broadway Elizabethan Cottages c1955 B222049

Broadway is the major tourist centre of the north Cotswolds, and looking at these Elizabethan cottages its easy to see why. Many jobs on the land were still labour intensive, and these little abodes would have been no luxury to live in before the age of second homes and improvement grants. If the man stooping is mowing the grass with such a tiny machine, he'll have his work cut out along with the grass!

Broadway ▶
The Tower c1955
B222054
The tower, built in 1799 for the Earl of Coventry, dominates the escarpment at Fish Hill. It is 65 feet high and situated at 1024 feet, the second highest point on the Cotswolds, giving a view to 12 counties from its top. During coaching days it was necessary to attach extra horses to climb Fish Hill on the way to London. The pre-Raphaelite artist and craftsman William Morris lived in the Cotswolds, which perhaps inspired him to form the Society for the Protection of Ancient Buildings.

▼ Charlton Kings, Cirencester Road c1955 C445001
Charlton Kings is now really a south-eastern suburb of Cheltenham on the busy A40 trunk road. This view is on the quieter A435 Cirencester Road. The neat 1930s semi-detached villas face the late Victorian terraced dwellings without the blight of parked cars and street sign clutter of today.

▲ Charlton Kings Glimpsed from Charlyon Hill c1955
C445004
Charlton Kings is overshadowed to the east by the high escarpment towering some 600 feet above it; in this view it can be seen nestling beyond the farmhouse.

**◄ Charlton Kings
Leckhampton Hill from
Lilley-Brook Golf Course
c1955** C445008
The gaunt escarpment,
including Leckhampton
Hill, broods over the golf
course just to the west of
the Cirencester Road.

Chipping Campden, Church Street and the Almshouses c1935 C335005
In the eyes of many, this is the finest Cotswold town. It is set in a slight valley on the high northern wolds, and is full of old houses; they include the late 14th-century Grevel's House, a 17th-century Market Hall and the remains of Campden House, burnt in 1645. The church, one of the finest wool churches, is built in Perpendicular style and dedicated to St James. The almshouses were built (in the plan form of a capital letter J in deference to King James) in 1612 for 12 people - 6 poor men and 6 poor women. The town became the focus for gathering and marketing wool. 'Chipping' derives from the old English for market.

Chipping Campden, Old Campden House and St James' Church c1955 C335016
The 120-foot tower of St James' dominates this view from the south-east. The church is notable for its 15th-century frontals, which are said to be the earliest set in the country. Among several fine brasses is an outstanding one to William Grevel, who died in 1401. A mile north-west of here is the Dover's Hill viewpoint, where the famous Cotswold games were formerly held.

**Chipping Campden
High Street c1945** C335028
The pleasing curve northwards of the High Street brings
our eyes to the tower of St James'. On the left is the
Market Hall, built in 1627 by Sir Baptist Hicks. From its
open bays, traders sold poultry, butter and cheese.

Chipping Campden High Street c1950
C335034
Looking down the High Street from the church, we see yet another attractive vista, with no street signs shouting. It is safe to cycle, and there is time for women to meet and talk about all that mattered then. The little boy, hand on hip, looks as if he would rather be on his way - or perhaps he has spotted the photographer in the middle of this quiet road.

◄ **Cleeve Hill, The Post Office c1940** C115002
Cleeve Hill, at 1080 feet above sea level, is the highest point of the Cotswolds. The A46 road climbs up from Cheltenham (about 900 feet below the summit) on its way to Winchcombe and Stratford upon Avon. No doubt copies of this print were sold as postcards in the post office. The escarpment can be glimpsed to the left.

◄ Chipping Campden The Eight Bells 1958

C335041

The ashlar stone-faced elevation of the Eight Bells is pleasing; note the trim projecting bay window. Also note that one of the hand bells on the support beam of the sign is missing - so perhaps it should be called the Seven Bells.

▼ Cleeve Hill, The Rising Sun Hotel c1940

C115003

Doubtless the owners of the Rover and Austin cars are refreshing themselves and marvelling at the view westwards across the Vale.

◄ Cleeve Hill Nottingham Hill and the Golf Course c1955

C115012

An Iron Age hill fort has been discovered near the summit of Cleeve Hill, and its ditches and ramparts can be found in the environment of a golf course. Nottingham Hill, also with a hill fort on its summit, is visible in the background. There are also remains of an ancient entrenchment 350 yards long on a part of the hill called Cleeve Cloud.

◄ **Cranham, The View towards the Church c1965** C179049
The village lies east of the A46 Stroud-Cheltenham road. The tower of St James' Church, built in the 1400s with two pairs of sheep shears carved into the stonework, is just visible. The village is seen against the backdrop of the escarpment clothed in woodland.

◀ **Cleeve Hill Courtauld's Convalescent Home c1960** C115024
Although the philanthropy of providing a convalescent home is to be applauded, it is difficult to applaud the planning authority's decision to allow a bland flat-roofed extension dating from the early 1950s.

▼ **Cranham, The Old House c1960** C179059
This building is in the centre of the village. The dates of 1687 and 1727 are carved on the door lintel, and it is typical of domestic architecture of the time. Note the bold drip courses and mullions of the gable windows.

◀ **Cranham, The Village c1960** C179061
We see here how Cotswold villages climbed up the valley sides as they grew, giving a terraced effect.

Dursley, Kingshill c1947 D72013
Dursley is the birthplace of Edward Fox, Bishop of Hereford, who introduced Thomas Cranmer to Henry VIII. This market town is situated in a valley between two spurs at the southern end of the escarpment looking across the Vale of Berkeley to the River Severn. This view of the northern suburb of Kingshill exudes 1930s suburbia. The cinema is showing 'Dark Passage' starring Humphrey Bogart and Lauren Bacall, bringing a touch of Hollywood to a small provincial town.

Dursley, Silver Street, c1947 D72019
Leading away from the Market Place (the Market House is visible in the distance) is Silver Street. The posters on the corner shop are advertising 'Dark Passage', noted in the Kingshill view. The venerable Austin Seven must be about twenty years old at the time of this photograph. The sign for the Star Inn evokes more of an image of the wild west than west country.

Dursley
Parsonage Street c1947 D72022
The Bargain Centre looks inviting, but the Castle Hotel
does not look much of a fortress. Parsonage Street leads
the eye to the wooded slopes of the escarpment beyond.
The buildings have Victorian and later shop fronts inserted
into their 18th- and 19th-century facades. The Ford van of
Burtons the grocers waits to deliver customer orders. It
appears to be a long way from its original home, judging
by the Nottingham registration number plate.

▼ **Dursley, Market House c1947** D72028

Dursley was once a wool and cloth manufacturing town of some importance. Flemish weavers settled here from what is now modern Belgium. This quaint yellow Market House stands on 12 arches; it was erected in 1738. The upper storey was used as a town hall, whilst market business was conducted on the open arcade of the ground floor. Local people were grateful to Queen Anne for money given to rebuild the church tower, and so they placed a statue of that good queen in the upper storey niche.

▼ **Dursley, Broadwell Terrace c1947** D72030

The medieval building on the right badly needed restoration fifty years ago - the stonework of the lunette-headed windows was badly decayed.

▲ **Dursley, Parsonage Stre**
c1947 D72035

This is the Market Place e of Parsonage Street, with a back view of the Market House and its cupola (containing one bell); the tower of St James appears behind. In January 1699 t spire and part of the steep fell down, and tragically some people were killed. Apparently bells were bei rung to celebrate repairs t the medieval structure, ani the stresses of the encirclir bells proved too much. Th tower was rebuilt in 1707 09 (without a spire!) and was based on the style of Colerne in adjacent Wiltshire. It was designed by a Thomas Sumsion, a famous mason who came from Colerne.

◀ **Dursley, Long Street c1947** D72031
The escarpment forms a good backdrop to this view. Long Street is considered the most architecturally distinguished street in town. Georges, the Bristol brewers, own the brick-built Old Bell Hotel, which dates back to the 18th century. Bristol is only around 15 miles away, and so exerts some influence on this town.

◀ **Dursley, Bull Pitch c1950** D72050
Bull Street leads the eye to the escarpment on the south side of the town. A fine example of an 18th-century townhouse is on the right; the pavement is raised up causeway-fashion above the carriageway.

◄ Dursley, Union Street c1950 D72042
The narrow steeply-sloping Union Street, east of the church of St James, leads the eye northward out of town and towards the stark ridge of Peaked Down; its visible notch gives the down its name.

▼ Hailes, The Abbey c1960 H5036
These ruined windows and arches are the remains of the cloisters. Situated in the north-west Cotswolds, Hailes Abbey was founded in 1246. The monks were of the Cistercian order, and one of their treasured possessions was a glass phial said to be filled with the Holy Blood. A shrine was built, and the Abbey became a focus for medieval pilgrims. The Abbey was dissolved on Christmas Eve 1539 and soon decayed. Stone was removed for buildings elsewhere.

◄ Painswick, New Street c1950 P3011
This is another exceptional little town, set in its own south-facing timbered valley just east of the escarpment between Stroud and Gloucester. It is a place that makes grey look very good. Local quarries around this hilly domain provided the grey limestone for fine buildings like the Old Grey Courthouse with its tall chimneys, attractive lines and gables. The stream water was used to power cloth mills. The pure water was also suited for dyeing cloth. The Falcon Inn dates from the early 1700s - it has a date stone of 1711. On the right we can spot examples of the topiary for which the town is famous.

◀ **Painswick, The Cross c1965** P3029
Here we see pleasant examples of 18th-century domestic architecture, but it looks in need of some re pointing. The Apothecary's and Shetland Wool shops look most inviting, with their charming windows.

◀ **Painswick
The Royal William
Hotel c1950** P3019
The hotel maintains
the old coaching
tradition by
displaying bus
timetables on its
fence. The lady in
the centre looks as
if she is awaiting the
bus, but the group
on the left give the
distinct impression
that they have been
turned out after
lunchtime closing.
Painswick is on the
main road from
Bath northwards to
Cheltenham, so it
has many inns for
travellers.

Painswick, The Lychgate c1965 P3039 ▲
The lychgate at the entrance to the churchyard of St Mary was built one hundred
years ago. Redolent of ancient times, the timber work came from the former bell
frame. The barge boards have carved outlines of bells, and the plastered panels
are inscribed: 'My Soul Doth Magnify the Lord; Jesus Christ my Saviour; Rejoiced
in God; my Spirit Hath. On the right we can glimpse the churchyard yew trees,
said to number 99 because the devil kills off the hundredth.

◀ **Painswick
The Stocks c1965** P3038
These substantial wrought iron
stocks are situated by the
entrance to the church yard,
and date from the 1840s. A
handrail has been considerably
placed by the stone seat.

▼ **Cranham, The Bells at Prinknash Abbey c1960** C179046

Prinknash (pronounced 'Prinash') is sited just west of the Stroud-Cheltenham Road. Used as a hunting lodge by the Abbot of Gloucester, it dates from the middle ages. Sold after the Dissolution, it became a private house. Prince Rupert used it in 1643 as his headquarters while directing the Royalist siege of Gloucester. Around 80 years ago, its then Catholic owner invited Benedictine monks to move their community here from Caldy Island (off the Pembrokeshire Coast). A new monastery building was begun in the late 1930s, and it took over 30 years to complete. The building is faced with square-cut Cotswold stone, and is unrelenting in its modernity. Digging the foundations exposed clay beds suited to making high-quality pottery for world markets. The bells are usually hung in the open air, as seen here, rather than in the tower steeple; they are chimed rather than rung.

▼ **Bisley, The Seven Springs c1955** B110001

This is the source of the River Churn, situated high up on the Western escarpment above Cheltenham. The Churn winds southward through Cirencester to join the River Thames near to Cricklade. Some people claim that Seven Springs is the source of the Thames, rather than Thameshead 11 miles south.

▲ **Stroud, The Town Centre c1950** S224016

A winding twisting slope leads up past Halfords to the Greyhound Inn on this busy thoroughfare through the town. A sign on the wall directs us to Halford cycle stores, a place so different from the company's modern superstore. A little Morris Z van in the newly nationalised G P O telephone green livery is parked by the kerb. So much has changed so quickly; but Stroud is still full of old character, with old wool mills dotted about the vicinity, reminders of its once major role. Deep valleys meet here, making the shape of a five pointed star. The waters powered corn mills in the Middle Ages, and later cloth and fulling mills; a map from 1824 shows over 150 mills in the area.

◄ **Stroud
The Town Centre
c1950** S224014
The Frith photographer has stepped back and swung his camera right of photograph No S224016, giving us a good view of the substantial ashlar stone-faced Greyhound Inn. There does not seem to be much traffic for this high-collared constable, so perhaps he is just posing, along with the uniformed man on the kerbside. No doubt this route through to Cheltenham and Gloucester had its busy moments.

Stroud, High Street c1950 S224020
The town's hilly character is noticeable here in this sloping High Street view. Those shop fronts look rather splendid, though Millwards seems a little empty, presenting rather a contrast to Curry's; they were then also in the cycle business, because it was so popular among tourers and for transport to work. Down the hill on the left we see another long-lost business, Timothy Whites, which disappeared when Boots gobbled it up.

Stroud
King Street c1950 S224011
King Street's early 19th-century buildings have acquired new shop fronts. The large premises of the multiple tailor's was rebuilt in the early 1930s in their corporate style. At £4 15s 0d, their suits were a bargain at just over half the price of bespoke garments: as their advertisements said, 'You can't beat Burton tailoring'. You could celebrate your wise purchase with a game of billiards and partake of refreshment at the Luciana Billiards Club upstairs.

Stroud, George Street c1950 S224013
Stroud's steep sloping streets are typified by this scene, which shows Russell Street branching right and George Street to the left. The 18th- and 19th-century buildings have benefited from new shop fronts. Note the substantial clock tower with its fluted corner columns.

Stroud, The Subscription Rooms c1950 S224015
The Subscription Rooms were built in 1833 in a fine Classical style with four imposing pillars. On the right we catch a glimpse of the Congregational Hall from the same era. The Ritz Cinema poster advertises 'The Four Feathers', starring John Clements and Ralph Richardson.

Stroud, High Street c1960 S224062
The shopping centre is buzzing with ladies displaying typical late 1950s fashions. The Ford Thames Trader lorry and Morris J-type van look too big for the carriageway. The curious little sign for Mac Fisheries is prominent in the left foreground, and on the opposite side of the road a shop sells Crown wallpaper, reminding us that the masses no longer have to put up with distemper on their walls and linoleum on the floor.

◀ **Stroud, The Bowling Green, Stratford Park c1955** S224007
Stratford Park is a northern suburb of Stroud. Here two neat pavilions overlook a busy bowling green. the omnipresent escarpment is in the background.

Stroud, The Shambles c1965 S224067

The town hall in the Shambles (named after the butchers quarters of the Middle Ages) was built in the late 1500s. The long arcade of cast iron fronts the Church Institute, and we can see the parish church of St Laurence, which was rebuilt from a 14th-century structure in the 1860s.

Uley, The Tumulus c1960 U3008

Uley's history precedes the Romans: nearby, a well-known long barrow known as 'Hetty Pegler's Tump' was uncovered. It was excavated twice in the early 19th century, and 15 human skeletons were found. The entrance, seen here, was reconstructed 150 years ago, and leads into a gallery with side chambers.

Uley, The Green and the Church c1965 U3010

Although only a village, Uley, just north of Dursley, was as famous as Stroud for its wool dyeing, specialising in a blue colour. This pleasant outlook, photographed from the Green, shows the parish church of St Giles, which was rebuilt almost 150 years ago. The Old Crown Inn on the left dates from the 18th century.

◄ **Uley, The Street c1965**
U3016
We are looking in the opposite direction from No U3011. Shadow falls across the pavement and the chatting mums, and the roadside filling station reflects an age when even the name of the fuel had dignity. The long arm hanging over the pumps used to swing round to the vehicles waiting in the street. Imagine the road rage if there were such obstructions today.

◄ Uley, The Street c1965

U3011

This view looks south down the hill to the village. The churchyard is on the right, and the wooded ridge of the spur south of Dursley flows across the horizon.

▼ Uley, The Green c1965

U3026

The Green has attractive Georgian houses - note the fine portico and parapet of High House on the left. Went House is in the centre. The narrow road on the right leads to the hamlet of Owlpen, and is called Fiery Lane.

◄ Winchcombe, North Street c1950 W378004

This old wool town is situated north of Cheltenham in the deep valley of the River Isbourne. Unusually, this river flows north to join the River Avon at Evesham; most Cotswold rivers flow south-east to join the Thames. In Saxon times, Winchcombe was the capital of the Mercian kingdom; the famous King Offa founded an abbey here. Winchcombe Abbey became one of the largest landowners in the Cotswolds. In medieval times it became a place of pilgrimage - the murdered St Kenelm was buried here. In the 17th century, an attempt to replace the declining wool trade with tobacco was thwarted by parliament because they thought it would disadvantage the North American Colonies. The White Lion Inn on the left dates from this period.

Winchcombe, Abbey Terrace c1955 W378025
Nothing remains of the Abbey. After the dissolution, the stonework was used to refurbish Sudeley Castle and for the buildings of the town. Abbey Terrace commemorates its name, along with a war memorial to those whose sacrifice for the greater good must also be remembered. We can see quite a large list for such a small town on the three sides facing the camera.

Winchcombe, High Street c1950 W378007
It is the calm before the storm of the modern motor age, though a delivery lorry on the bend presents quite an obstruction. This is still very much the age of the bicycle, as we can see from all those parked two-wheelers. The ashlar stone building with a Cotswold-tiled mansard roof, on the left, contrasts with the half-timbered White Hart Hotel down on the right and with the well-proportioned three-storey building situated on the curve.

Winchcombe
High Street c1955 W378024
The John Wesley Cafe dates from the 16th century, although its concession to mid 20th-century life was to display a Coca Cola sign. The half-timbered George Hotel, although much altered subsequently, is a most interesting building; it is believed to be pre-Reformation, and was used as an inn by the pilgrims to the Abbey. As we can easily see, this is Church Fete weekend - luckily, it is a warm summer day.

◀ **Winchcombe, Hailes Street c1955** W378022
This is a continuation of the High Street. The half-timbered building on the left dates from Tudor times. Two ladies are seen exchanging gossip on a warm sunny afternoon, while in the distance a weary man pushes his bicycle up the gentle slope into town.

**◄ Winchcombe
The Church from
Almsbury Farm
c1950** W378008
The parish church of
St Peter was built in
the 1460s and is one
of the great Cotswold
wool churches,
although it is not quite
so ornate as some.
There are holes from
musket bullets caused
when Royalist
prisoners were shot
during the Civil War.
The church is also
famous for around 40
grotesque gargoyle
carvings known as the
Winchcombe
Worthies.

**Woodchester ►
The Valley c1960**
W130502
This delightful view
shows Woodchester
sprawled across the
slope, with a country
lane in the foreground
twisting and turning as
it climbs up the
valley side.

**◄ Woodchester
The Monastery c1960**
W130005
The village of Woodchester
is well down in a valley
leading north to Stroud.
This view shows the
western valley slopes
scattered with its houses.
A large Roman villa was
discovered around 200
years ago, and a fine
mosaic floor was found
in one of the 60 rooms.
In the late 1840s, the
Dominican Priory of Our
Lady of the Annunciation
was built in the Decorated
architectural style.

Cirencester

Cirencester, Cricklade Street c1950 C106010
Roman armies invaded Britain in AD 43, moving
north-west. They founded their town of Corinium
by the River Churn, in an area occupied by a
native tribe called Dobunni. Corinium became an
important town at the junction of the Fosse Way
and Ermine and Akeman Streets. The town was
mostly destroyed by the Saxons; the Normans built
a large abbey which prospered until the
dissolution, but growth continued as a market,
particularly in the wool trade. This view shows
Cricklade Street, which leads out of the Market
Place. Its architecture has succumbed to a hotch
potch of shop fronts, with F R Smith's displaying
lettering in the style of 1930s modernism.

Cirencester, Gloucester Street c1950 C106011

A fine 17th-century dwelling dominates this view. To the left, A J Burton sold toys and confectionery - doubtless a very popular shop with children. Next door was C Rowe's glass, earthenware and general store, patronised more by their parents.

Cirencester, The Park Drive c1950 C106013

From the avenue lined with lime trees the eye is drawn eastwards to the 162-foot high tower of St John the Baptist's, the tallest tower in Gloucestershire, containing a ring of twelve bells with the tenor weighing 26 cwt (over 1.25 metric tonnes).

Cirencester, The Church and the Town Hall c1950 C106014
The magnificent three-storey porch, England's largest and constructed 100 years after the tower, faces the Market Square. The tower soaring above was begun in c1400 in Perpendicular style; it was originally intended to have a spire, but structural settlement occurred and buttresses had to be incorporated. It is the largest church in Gloucestershire. The less mighty shop building next door advertises Hunt Tailors. We can see a lady shopper out in trousers, which would have been frowned on before the war.

▼ **Cirencester, The Fleece Hotel and Dyer Street c1950** C106016
The Fleece Hotel, facing the Market Square, is of two different styles. On the left, the 17th-century stucco front has been painted to give the effect of half-timbering, whilst to the right is an 18th-century Georgian building containing the carriage entrance to the yard. The Georgian architectural style continues on both sides of Dyer Street. On the right, Curry's emphasise their main interest in bicycles rather than in electrical goods, which were yet to boom with pop music, television and labour-saving devices to liberate the housewife. Their splendid Gloucester-registered Austin delivery van stands ready for its orders, untroubled by parking restrictions or ubiquitous traffic wardens.

▼ **Cirencester, Castle Street c1950** C106018
The architecture of the Post Office and W H Smith is the commercial equivalent of the vernacular style of the town. The bulk of the Post Office gives the necessary impression of security, and Smith's signboard is refreshingly different from the modern corporate image now deemed indispensable.

▲ **Cirencester, Castle Street c1950** C106046
Here we view the street from the opposite direction to picture No C106018, gaining a better view of W H Smith and two well-known banks on the right. Lloyds building was originally a wool merchant's house, becoming a bank in the 1790s. It is considered to be the town's finest example of Palladian architecture of the early 17th century.

◄ **Cirencester, Gloucester Street c1950** C106019
Cottages in indigenous style lead up to the bend and a pleasing old gas lamp standard. Drainage enthusiasts will appreciate the guttering passing the windows, which eliminates the need for many down pipes but makes opening windows difficult! The large gabled building, centre right, was built nearly 100 years ago for the Bathurst Estate, and so is not as old as it looks.

Cirencester, The Memorial Hospital c1950 C106034
There was no problem in parking in front of the Memorial Cottage Hospital 50 years ago; the large Vauxhall and the smaller Standard stand behind the tulips in this spring scene. The building is fairly plain, but note the turned brick chimney stacks with their ornate stone capping, and the ogee-turned finial to the barge boards.

Cirencester, The Armoury c1950 C106035
Although it looks like a medieval castle, this building was only built in 1857; it was barracks for the Royal Gloucester Militia Armoury.

The Southern Cotswolds

Bibury
Arlington Row c1950 B530001
Bibury, Gloucestershire is situated in the eastern wolds
on the River Coln beside the A433 Burford to
Cirencester road. An attractive village with a fine church,
Saxon to Early English, it is popular with tourists. William
Morris called it: 'the most beautiful village in England'.
Here the little river backwater trickles by in a scene
of tranquillity on a sunny day in late spring.

▼ **Bibury, Arlington Mill c1955** B530021
The mill was built in the 17th century on a site dating back to Domesday. It was used both as a cloth and a corn mill. The cottage projecting out towards the road was an 18th-century addition. The stone piers and buttresses were added in the 1850s, together with wrought iron strengthening beams and columns.

▼ **Bibury, Arlington Row c1955** B530022
Originally a monastic sheephouse, these cottages were converted into weavers' dwellings in the 17th century, and are now owned by the National Trust. Woven cloth was taken to the mill for fulling. There is a water meadow to the right of the river.

▲ **Bibury, The Swan Hotel and the Bridge c1955**
B530030
The present Swan Hotel was built in the 18th century on the site of an earlier inn, and was extended some 70 years ago. The river Colne, flowing south-east to its confluence with the Thames at Lechlade 10 miles away, has captivated this old countryman and boy.

◄ **Chalford**
The Hill c1960 C569011
Chalford is situated in the Golden Valley to the east of Stroud, an industrial area even in the middle ages, with water-powered corn and fulling mills. This expanded with the industrial revolution: the narrow base to the steep-sided valley contains the Thames-Severn Canal, the Swindon-Gloucester railway line and the river Frome. The village is sited on the north face of the valley, and the terracing of the housing is clearly seen.

◄ **Duntisbourne Abbots, The Church c1960**
D161010
The church of St Peter, with its unusual saddleback-roofed tower, dates from Norman times. It belonged to St Peter's Abbey in Gloucester during the Middle Ages - hence the suffix Abbots.

Duntisbourne Abbots
The Village c1960
D161004
Duntisbourne Abbots is the largest of the Duntisbourne villages - the others are Duntisbourne Leer, Middle Duntisbourne and Duntisbourne Rouse. They are all situated on the small River Dunt, which flows into the River Churn just north of Cirencester. This tranquil view typifies the best in Cotswold villages.

Duntisbourne Abbots
The Ford c1960 D161012
The river Dunt has been diverted to run alongside the road. It was doubtless used to swell up the felloes of cart and wagon wheels, for in hot, dry weather they contracted, and the metal tyres became loose. The stretch of water was also convenient to water livestock.

Duntisbourne Abbots
The Youth Hostel
c1960 D161501
This large dwelling is just north of the church, and was ideal for conversion into a youth hostel. The couple approaching on bicycles look ready for the hostel's refreshment and comfortable beds before continuing their tour.

◀ **Fairford, The Market Place c1958** F145024
This view of the square shows little change in the thirteen years interim after photograph No F145003, though the ivy creeper has gone from the dwelling on the far right. But the cars are getting bigger, and the Vauxhall exudes the post-war General Motors influence - Britain is going to get a lot more American yet! We also see our first caravan of this book: there will be a lot more over the years, as people seek cheap mobile holidays.

◀ **Fairford, The Square c1945** F145003

Fairford is situated on the River Coln a few miles from the Thames in Gloucestershire. It is noted for fishing, and for a fine old mill dating from a long-time dependency on wool. It was the birthplace of the Oxford Tractarian Movement's leading light, John Keble, in 1792. No doubt his zealous outlook was inspired by the fine 15th- and 16th-century church. Although very much a stone-built place, it lacks the Cotswold atmosphere of the settlements on the high wold. The Market Place, shown here, has fine 17th- and 18th-century buildings; the 3-storey ashlar-faced house right of centre is a fine example, with its rusticated ground floor stonework, fine pediment and cornice.

▼ **Fairford, The Mill c1965**
F145036

The mill stands on the northern edge of town, with St Mary's graveyard visible beyond; it dates from Norman times, and by the Middle Ages was used for fulling cloth. The church was rebuilt by a rich wool merchant and his son in the late 1400s. It is famous for its stained glass, which has miraculously survived for 500 years; 28 windows tell the Christian story, and are known as 'the poor man's bible'.

◀ **Lechlade, The Old Market Place c1950** L147011

Lechlade, situated on the river Thames, is the gateway to the Cotswolds from the south-east. The Cotswold rivers of Coln and Leach join the Thames here, and the town is much influenced by them. Lechlade stone was used to build St Paul's Cathedral; it was brought from 10 miles north down to Taynton Quarry. The town is dominated by the Market Place and the church of St Lawrence. The 18th-century stone building of the Lion pub looks snug, and the 3-storey red brick New Inn can be glimpsed on the corner.

Lechlade, St John's Lock c1955 L147024
Lechlade is the highest lock on the River Thames; it is seen here from St John's bridge. The lock keeper's neat and tidy cottage garden is noteworthy, as is the view across the water meadows to the steeple of St Lawrence's church.

Lechlade, The Wharf c1955 L147034
Commercial traffic on the Thames virtually ceased a hundred years ago, and today pleasure boating is everything. There was a lull during the Second World War, but here, soon after, we see early signs of revival. The small boatyard on the right is surrounded with corrugated iron-clad buildings, whilst the stone building in the centre proclaims tea gardens on a gable sign, ready for business on this early spring day.

Lechlade
The Square c1955 L147041
In this view of the eastern side of the
Market Place, the old vicarage takes pride
of place. It was built in 1805. Note the
mansard roof and the bull's eye window
above the two-storey entrance porch.

▼ Lechlade, Riverside Tea Gardens c1955 L147049

Spring sunshine on the river is tempting out these rowers. Perhaps the lady should be paying less attention to the photographer and more to where her boat is going. Meanwhile a canoe stands ready on the slipway, and a man takes a photo of his own.

▼ Lechlade, The River c1955 L147052

The 18th-century Ha'Penny Bridge is finely complimented by the sailing craft emerging from the semi-circle of its wide arch, thus catching the eye of what looks like Bill Syke's dog. All this charm is viewed from the tea garden on the north bank. The small squat Toll House can be seen over the parapet.

▲ Lechlade, The Church from the River c1955

L147057

Here we have a perfect view of St Lawrence's church from across the Thames. This is another wool church, dating from the late 1400s. The stone came from Taynton Quarry near Burford about 10 miles away; as we have mentioned already, it supplied St Paul's cathedral and many Oxford buildings.

◀ **Lechlade, Burford Street c1950** L147063
This street of fine Georgian buildings leads northwards from the Market Place. The sign of the Tudor Swan Hotel could not match the elegance of the bird in picture No L147057, but it looks a good hotel. Note the Jaguar car parked under the Union Flag far right: alas, Jaguars are no longer British.

Minchinhampton High Street c1960
M83046
This small, attractive market town is situated on a hilltop spur of the western escarpment between Nailsworth and Stroud. Its 18th-century cloth trade was hectic, and its stone quarry produced high-grade material. Looking into the distance, we see a High Street building from the 18th century in the centre, with four stone vases as finials to the parapet. The truncated spire of Holy Trinity church is seen on the skyline: the medieval spire was reduced to its present level and capped with an unusual coronet of stone in 1563 because it was in danger of collapse.

Minchinhampton, The Market House c1960   M83058
The Market House, built in 1698, dominates the Square. External pillars are stone, but inside they are timber - we can just glimpse one of them. The Crown Hotel in the background dates from the 18th century, and we can see a splendid row of 9 sash windows at first-floor level.

Minchinhampton Tom Long's Post c1960
M83060
The common lies just west of the town, and is around 600 feet above sea level. This windswept place high up on the escarpment has a prehistoric Long Barrow. Six minor roads intersect at a spot called Long Tom's Post, so called in spite of the County Council sign naming it Tom Long's Post. Some say that Long Tom was a highwayman hung at this spot. Others say that a suicide was buried here.

◄ **Nailsworth**
The Trout Hatcheries c1955
N1007
Nailsworth is situated in two steep tree-lined valleys, one coming from the east containing the Tetbury road, and the other the A46 road north from Bath. The valleys both contain streams which merge to form the Nailsworth River Avon. The streams have gone from powering mills to being used as trout hatcheries.

▼ **Nailsworth, Shortwood c1955** N1010
Shortwood, a western suburb of Nailsworth, occupies an area at the top of the valley above the steep lower slopes. The small church dedicated to All Saints can be seen on the horizon on the left. Although 13th-century in style, it was only built in the 1860s.

▼ **Nailsworth, The Clock Tower c1955** N1056
This clock tower was erected at the junction of the Bath and Tetbury roads in 1951, to commemorate the Festival of Britain. In the background the steep valley side is covered with tree growth; through it houses can be glimpsed at varying levels.

▲ **Nailsworth, From Bath Road c1955** N1060
Here we see the A46 Bath Road descending the hill toward the valley bottom, where the Tetbury road merges. In the centre is the church of St George, which was built just over a hundred years ago and which still awaits its tower and spire. Again, the wooded valley side forms a backdrop.

◄ **South Cerney
The Village c1960** S517006
The settlement lies on the
River Churn just before
its confluence with the
Thames. Here one of the
typical low-arched bridges
can be seen with its
stonework recently
re-pointed.

South Cerney, The Church c1960 S517008
The River Churn is in the foreground. This fine church dates from Norman times; it has a central tower, and one time a spire, which was dismantled during the 1862 restoration. The large, plain 18th-century three-storey Manor House can be glimpsed beyond the yew tree in the churchyard.

South Cerney, The Memorial c1960 S517013
This well-cared-for memorial is at the end of Broadway Lane; it lists the names of those who left these sleepy parts for an experience of unbelievable violence, carnage and sacrifice.

Tetbury
Long Street c1950 T155016
This is another delightful town, which stands on the main
Cirencester-Bath road. Long Street reveals fine examples of
17th-century architecture. The building with four gables has
unusual castellated heads to its bay windows.

◄ **Tetbury, Bath Road c1955** T155028
The attractive entrance to the town is seen here; we are looking north from Bath. The parish church of St Mary stands boldly on its mound. It was rebuilt in 1781, and the tower and spire were rebuilt a hundred years later. Note the huge size of the windows.

**Tetbury
The Chipping c1955**
T155025
The fine house on the right dates from the 18th century, and has a splendid veranda and balcony of wrought iron added in the 1800s.

Tetbury, Chipping Steps c1965 T155076
This street dates from medieval times. Notice how the 16th-century and later buildings step down to accommodate the change in level.

Tetbury, Westonbirt School c1965 T155063
Something of a palace, Westonbirt was built nearly 150 years ago in Elizabethan style, and remains in fine condition. The details speak volumes for the architect Lewis Vulliamy (who also designed town houses for London's Park Lane) and for the craftsmanship of the masons and carpenters. Roughly 3 miles from Tetbury, it is now a girls' school.

Tetbury, Church Street c1960 T155050
The street has been commercialised, with shop fronts inserted into 17th-century buildings. It is believed that the stucco render probably hides timber work. Note how the Eight Bells Inn projects over the pavement.

Tetbury, Market Place c1960 T155059
The Market House was built in 1655; it is a substantial building supported on fat stone columns. Originally it would have been more striking, but the third storey was removed in 1817. Note the two gilded dolphins on the weathervane above the cupola. On the left is the White Hart Hotel, rebuilt in Jacobean style.

Index

Frith Book Co Titles

www.francisfrith.co.uk

The Frith Book Company publishes over 100 new titles each year. A selection of those currently available is listed below. For latest catalogue please contact Frith Book Co. **Town Books** 96 pages, approximately 100 photos. **County and Themed Books** 128 pages, approximately 150 photos (unless specified). All titles hardback with laminated case and jacket, except those indicated pb (paperback)

Title	ISBN	Price	Title	ISBN	Price
Amersham, Chesham & Rickmansworth (pb)	1-85937-340-2	£9.99	Devon (pb)	1-85937-297-x	£9.99
Andover (pb)	1-85937-292-9	£9.99	Devon Churches (pb)	1-85937-250-3	£9.99
Aylesbury (pb)	1-85937-227-9	£9.99	Dorchester (pb)	1-85937-307-0	£9.99
Barnstaple (pb)	1-85937-300-3	£9.99	Dorset (pb)	1-85937-269-4	£9.99
Basildon Living Memories (pb)	1-85937-515-4	£9.99	Dorset Coast (pb)	1-85937-299-6	£9.99
Bath (pb)	1-85937-419-0	£9.99	Dorset Living Memories (pb)	1-85937-584-7	£9.99
Bedford (pb)	1-85937-205-8	£9.99	Down the Severn (pb)	1-85937-560-x	£9.99
Bedfordshire Living Memories	1-85937-513-8	£14.99	Down The Thames (pb)	1-85937-278-3	£9.99
Belfast (pb)	1-85937-303-8	£9.99	Down the Trent	1-85937-311-9	£14.99
Berkshire (pb)	1-85937-191-4	£9.99	East Anglia (pb)	1-85937-265-1	£9.99
Berkshire Churches	1-85937-170-1	£17.99	East Grinstead (pb)	1-85937-138-8	£9.99
Berkshire Living Memories	1-85937-332-1	£14.99	East London	1-85937-080-2	£14.99
Black Country	1-85937-497-2	£12.99	East Sussex (pb)	1-85937-606-1	£9.99
Blackpool (pb)	1-85937-393-3	£9.99	Eastbourne (pb)	1-85937-399-2	£9.99
Bognor Regis (pb)	1-85937-431-x	£9.99	Edinburgh (pb)	1-85937-193-0	£8.99
Bournemouth (pb)	1-85937-545-6	£9.99	England In The 1880s	1-85937-331-3	£17.99
Bradford (pb)	1-85937-204-x	£9.99	Essex - Second Selection	1-85937-456-5	£14.99
Bridgend (pb)	1-85937-386-0	£7.99	Essex (pb)	1-85937-270-8	£9.99
Bridgwater (pb)	1-85937-305-4	£9.99	Essex Coast	1-85937-342-9	£14.99
Bridport (pb)	1-85937-327-5	£9.99	Essex Living Memories	1-85937-490-5	£14.99
Brighton (pb)	1-85937-192-2	£8.99	Exeter	1-85937-539-1	£9.99
Bristol (pb)	1-85937-264-3	£9.99	Exmoor (pb)	1-85937-608-8	£9.99
British Life A Century Ago (pb)	1-85937-213-9	£9.99	Falmouth (pb)	1-85937-594-4	£9.99
Buckinghamshire (pb)	1-85937-200-7	£9.99	Folkestone (pb)	1-85937-124-8	£9.99
Camberley (pb)	1-85937-222-8	£9.99	Frome (pb)	1-85937-317-8	£9.99
Cambridge (pb)	1-85937-422-0	£9.99	Glamorgan	1-85937-488-3	£14.99
Cambridgeshire (pb)	1-85937-420-4	£9.99	Glasgow (pb)	1-85937-190-6	£9.99
Cambridgeshire Villages	1-85937-523-5	£14.99	Glastonbury (pb)	1-85937-338-0	£7.99
Canals And Waterways (pb)	1-85937-291-0	£9.99	Gloucester (pb)	1-85937-232-5	£9.99
Canterbury Cathedral (pb)	1-85937-179-5	£9.99	Gloucestershire (pb)	1-85937-561-8	£9.99
Cardiff (pb)	1-85937-093-4	£9.99	Great Yarmouth (pb)	1-85937-426-3	£9.99
Carmarthenshire (pb)	1-85937-604-5	£9.99	Greater Manchester (pb)	1-85937-266-x	£9.99
Chelmsford (pb)	1-85937-310-0	£9.99	Guildford (pb)	1-85937-410-7	£9.99
Cheltenham (pb)	1-85937-095-0	£9.99	Hampshire (pb)	1-85937-279-1	£9.99
Cheshire (pb)	1-85937-271-6	£9.99	Harrogate (pb)	1-85937-423-9	£9.99
Chester (pb)	1-85937-382 8	£9.99	Hastings and Bexhill (pb)	1-85937-131-0	£9.99
Chesterfield (pb)	1-85937-378-x	£9.99	Heart of Lancashire (pb)	1-85937-197-3	£9.99
Chichester (pb)	1-85937-228-7	£9.99	Helston (pb)	1-85937-214-7	£9.99
Churches of East Cornwall (pb)	1-85937-249-x	£9.99	Hereford (pb)	1-85937-175-2	£9.99
Churches of Hampshire (pb)	1-85937-207-4	£9.99	Herefordshire (pb)	1-85937-567-7	£9.99
Cinque Ports & Two Ancient Towns	1-85937-492-1	£14.99	Herefordshire Living Memories	1-85937-514-6	£14.99
Colchester (pb)	1-85937-188-4	£8.99	Hertfordshire (pb)	1-85937-247-3	£9.99
Cornwall (pb)	1-85937-229-5	£9.99	Horsham (pb)	1-85937-432-8	£9.99
Cornwall Living Memories	1-85937-248-1	£14.99	Humberside (pb)	1-85937-605-3	£9.99
Cotswolds (pb)	1-85937-230-9	£9.99	Hythe, Romney Marsh, Ashford (pb)	1-85937-256-2	£9.99
Cotswolds Living Memories	1-85937-255-4	£14.99	Ipswich (pb)	1-85937-424-7	£9.99
County Durham (pb)	1-85937-398-4	£9.99	Isle of Man (pb)	1-85937-268-6	£9.99
Croydon Living Memories (pb)	1-85937-162-0	£9.99	Isle of Wight (pb)	1-85937-429-8	£9.99
Cumbria (pb)	1-85937-621-5	£9.99	Isle of Wight Living Memories	1-85937-304-6	£14.99
Derby (pb)	1-85937-367-4	£9.99	Kent (pb)	1-85937-189-2	£9.99
Derbyshire (pb)	1-85937-196-5	£9.99	Kent Living Memories(pb)	1-85937-401-8	£9.99
Derbyshire Living Memories	1-85937-330-5	£14.99	Kings Lynn (pb)	1-85937-334-8	£9.99

Available from your local bookshop or from the publisher

Frith Book Co Titles (continued)

Title	ISBN	Price	Title	ISBN	Price
Lake District (pb)	1-85937-275-9	£9.99	Sherborne (pb)	1-85937-301-1	£9.99
Lancashire Living Memories	1-85937-335-6	£14.99	Shrewsbury (pb)	1-85937-325-9	£9.99
Lancaster, Morecambe, Heysham (pb)	1-85937-233-3	£9.99	Shropshire (pb)	1-85937-326-7	£9.99
Leeds (pb)	1-85937-202-3	£9.99	Shropshire Living Memories	1-85937-643-6	£14.99
Leicester (pb)	1-85937-381-x	£9.99	Somerset	1-85937-153-1	£14.99
Leicestershire & Rutland Living Memories	1-85937-500-6	£12.99	South Devon Coast	1-85937-107-8	£14.99
Leicestershire (pb)	1-85937-185-x	£9.99	South Devon Living Memories (pb)	1-85937-609-6	£9.99
Lighthouses	1-85937-257-0	£9.99	South East London (pb)	1-85937-263-5	£9.99
Lincoln (pb)	1-85937-380-1	£9.99	South Somerset	1-85937-318-6	£14.99
Lincolnshire (pb)	1-85937-433-6	£9.99	South Wales	1-85937-519-7	£14.99
Liverpool and Merseyside (pb)	1-85937-234-1	£9.99	Southampton (pb)	1-85937-427-1	£9.99
London (pb)	1-85937-183-3	£9.99	Southend (pb)	1-85937-313-5	£9.99
London Living Memories	1-85937-454-9	£14.99	Southport (pb)	1-85937-425-5	£9.99
Ludlow (pb)	1-85937-176-0	£9.99	St Albans (pb)	1-85937-341-0	£9.99
Luton (pb)	1-85937-235-x	£9.99	St Ives (pb)	1-85937-415-8	£9.99
Maidenhead (pb)	1-85937-339-9	£9.99	Stafford Living Memories (pb)	1-85937-503-0	£9.99
Maidstone (pb)	1-85937-391-7	£9.99	Staffordshire (pb)	1-85937-308-9	£9.99
Manchester (pb)	1-85937-198-1	£9.99	Stourbridge (pb)	1-85937-530-8	£9.99
Marlborough (pb)	1-85937-336-4	£9.99	Stratford upon Avon (pb)	1-85937-388-7	£9.99
Middlesex	1-85937-158-2	£14.99	Suffolk (pb)	1-85937-221-x	£9.99
Monmouthshire	1-85937-532-4	£14.99	Suffolk Coast (pb)	1-85937-610-x	£9.99
New Forest (pb)	1-85937-390-9	£9.99	Surrey (pb)	1-85937-240-6	£9.99
Newark (pb)	1-85937-366-6	£9.99	Surrey Living Memories	1-85937-328-3	£14.99
Newport, Wales (pb)	1-85937-258-9	£9.99	Sussex (pb)	1-85937-184-1	£9.99
Newquay (pb)	1-85937-421-2	£9.99	Sutton (pb)	1-85937-337-2	£9.99
Norfolk (pb)	1-85937-195-7	£9.99	Swansea (pb)	1-85937-167-1	£9.99
Norfolk Broads	1-85937-486-7	£14.99	Taunton (pb)	1-85937-314-3	£9.99
Norfolk Living Memories (pb)	1-85937-402-6	£9.99	Tees Valley & Cleveland (pb)	1-85937-623-1	£9.99
North Buckinghamshire	1-85937-626-6	£14.99	Teignmouth (pb)	1-85937-370-4	£7.99
North Devon Living Memories	1-85937-261-9	£14.99	Thanet (pb)	1-85937-116-7	£9.99
North Hertfordshire	1-85937-547-2	£14.99	Tiverton (pb)	1-85937-178-7	£9.99
North London (pb)	1-85937-403-4	£9.99	Torbay (pb)	1-85937-597-9	£9.99
North Somerset	1-85937-302-x	£14.99	Truro (pb)	1-85937-598-7	£9.99
North Wales (pb)	1-85937-298-8	£9.99	Victorian & Edwardian Dorset	1-85937-254-6	£14.99
North Yorkshire (pb)	1-85937-236-8	£9.99	Victorian & Edwardian Kent (pb)	1-85937-624-X	£9.99
Northamptonshire Living Memories	1-85937-529-4	£14.99	Victorian & Edwardian Maritime Album (pb)	1-85937-622-3	£9.99
Northamptonshire	1-85937-150-7	£14.99	Victorian and Edwardian Sussex (pb)	1-85937-625-8	£9.99
Northumberland Tyne & Wear (pb)	1-85937-281-3	£9.99	Villages of Devon (pb)	1-85937-293-7	£9.99
Northumberland	1-85937-522-7	£14.99	Villages of Kent (pb)	1-85937-294-5	£9.99
Norwich (pb)	1-85937-194-9	£8.99	Villages of Sussex (pb)	1-85937-295-3	£9.99
Nottingham (pb)	1-85937-324-0	£9.99	Warrington (pb)	1-85937-507-3	£9.99
Nottinghamshire (pb)	1-85937-187-6	£9.99	Warwick (pb)	1-85937-518-9	£9.99
Oxford (pb)	1-85937-411-5	£9.99	Warwickshire (pb)	1-85937-203-1	£9.99
Oxfordshire (pb)	1-85937-430-1	£9.99	Welsh Castles (pb)	1-85937-322-4	£9.99
Oxfordshire Living Memories	1-85937-525-1	£14.99	West Midlands (pb)	1-85937-289-9	£9.99
Paignton (pb)	1-85937-374-7	£7.99	West Sussex (pb)	1-85937-607-x	£9.99
Peak District (pb)	1-85937-280-5	£9.99	West Yorkshire (pb)	1-85937-201-5	£9.99
Pembrokeshire	1-85937-262-7	£14.99	Weston Super Mare (pb)	1-85937-306-2	£9.99
Penzance (pb)	1-85937-595-2	£9.99	Weymouth (pb)	1-85937-209-0	£9.99
Peterborough (pb)	1-85937-219-8	£9.99	Wiltshire (pb)	1-85937-277-5	£9.99
Picturesque Harbours	1-85937-208-2	£14.99	Wiltshire Churches (pb)	1-85937-171-x	£9.99
Piers	1-85937-237-6	£17.99	Wiltshire Living Memories (pb)	1-85937-396-8	£9.99
Plymouth (pb)	1-85937-389-5	£9.99	Winchester (pb)	1-85937-428-x	£9.99
Poole & Sandbanks (pb)	1-85937-251-1	£9.99	Windsor (pb)	1-85937-333-x	£9.99
Preston (pb)	1-85937-212-0	£9.99	Wokingham & Bracknell (pb)	1-85937-329-1	£9.99
Reading (pb)	1-85937-238-4	£9.99	Woodbridge (pb)	1-85937-498-0	£9.99
Redhill to Reigate (pb)	1-85937-596-0	£9.99	Worcester (pb)	1-85937-165-5	£9.99
Ringwood (pb)	1-85937-384-4	£7.99	Worcestershire Living Memories	1-85937-489-1	£14.99
Romford (pb)	1-85937-319-4	£9.99	Worcestershire	1-85937-152-3	£14.99
Royal Tunbridge Wells (pb)	1-85937-504-9	£9.99	York (pb)	1-85937-199-x	£9.99
Salisbury (pb)	1-85937-239-2	£9.99	Yorkshire (pb)	1-85937-186-8	£9.99
Scarborough (pb)	1-85937-379-8	£9.99	Yorkshire Coastal Memories	1-85937-506-5	£14.99
Sevenoaks and Tonbridge (pb)	1-85937-392-5	£9.99	Yorkshire Dales	1-85937-502-2	£14.99
Sheffield & South Yorks (pb)	1-85937-267-8	£9.99	Yorkshire Living Memories (pb)	1-85937-397-6	£9.99

See Frith books on the internet at www.francisfrith.co.uk

FRITH PRODUCTS & SERVICES

Francis Frith would doubtless be pleased to know that the pioneering publishing venture he started in 1860 still continues today. Over a hundred and forty years later, The Francis Frith Collection continues in the same innovative tradition and is now one of the foremost publishers of vintage photographs in the world. Some of the current activities include:

Interior Decoration

Today Frith's photographs can be seen framed and as giant wall murals in thousands of pubs, restaurants, hotels, banks, retail stores and other public buildings throughout the country. In every case they enhance the unique local atmosphere of the places they depict and provide reminders of gentler days in an increasingly busy and frenetic world.

Product Promotions

Frith products are used by many major companies to promote the sales of their own products or to reinforce their own history and heritage. Frith promotions have been used by Hovis bread, Courage beers, Scots Porage Oats, Colman's mustard, Cadbury's foods, Mellow Birds coffee, Dunhill pipe tobacco, Guinness, and Bulmer's Cider.

Genealogy and Family History

As the interest in family history and roots grows world-wide, more and more people are turning to Frith's photographs of Great Britain for images of the towns, villages and streets where their ancestors lived; and, of course, photographs of the churches and chapels where their ancestors were christened, married and buried are an essential part of every genealogy tree and family album.

Frith Products

All Frith photographs are available Framed or just as Mounted Prints and Posters (size 23 x 16 inches). These may be ordered from the address below. From time to time other products - Address Books, Calendars, Table Mats, etc - are available.

The Internet

Already fifty thousand Frith photographs can be viewed and purchased on the internet through the Frith websites and a myriad of partner sites.

For more detailed information on Frith companies and products, look at these sites:

www.francisfrith.co.uk
www.francisfrith.com
(for North American visitors)

See the complete list of Frith Books at:

www.francisfrith.co.uk

This web site is regularly updated with the latest list of publications from the Frith Book Company. If you wish to buy books relating to another part of the country that your local bookshop does not stock, you may purchase on-line.

For further information, trade, or author enquiries please contact us at the address below:
The Francis Frith Collection, Frith's Barn, Teffont, Salisbury, Wiltshire, England SP3 5QP.
Tel: +44 (0)1722 716 376 Fax: +44 (0)1722 716 881 Email: sales@francisfrith.co.uk

See Frith books on the internet at www.francisfrith.co.uk

FREE MOUNTED PRINT

Mounted Print
Overall size 14 x 11 inches

Fill in and cut out this voucher and return
it with your remittance for £2.25 (to cover postage and handling). Offer valid for delivery to UK addresses only.

Choose any photograph included in this book.
Your SEPIA print will be A4 in size. It will be mounted in a cream mount with a burgundy rule line (overall size 14 x 11 inches).

**Order additional Mounted Prints
at HALF PRICE (only £7.49 each*)**
If you would like to order more Frith prints from this book, possibly as gifts for friends and family, you can buy them at half price (with no additional postage and handling costs).

Have your Mounted Prints framed
For an extra £14.95 per print* you can have your mounted print(s) framed in an elegant polished wood and gilt moulding, overall size 16 x 13 inches (no additional postage and handling required).

---

* IMPORTANT!

These special prices are only available if you order at the same time as you order your free mounted print. You must use the ORIGINAL VOUCHER on this page (no copies permitted). We can only despatch to one address.

Send completed Voucher form to:
The Francis Frith Collection, Frith's Barn, Teffont, Salisbury, Wiltshire SP3 5QP

Voucher for **FREE** and Reduced Price Frith Prints

Please do not photocopy this voucher. Only the original is valid, so please fill it in, cut it out and return it to us with your order.

Picture ref no	Page no	Qty	Mounted @ £7.49	Framed + £14.95	Total Cost
		1	Free of charge*	£	£
			£7.49	£	£
			£7.49	£	£
			£7.49	£	£
			£7.49	£	£
			£7.49	£	£

Please allow 28 days for delivery

* Post & handling (UK)	£2.25
Total Order Cost	£

Title of this book . . . .

I enclose a cheque/postal order for £ . . . . made payable to 'The Francis Frith Collection'

OR please debit my Mastercard / Visa / Switch / Amex card
(credit cards please on all overseas orders), details below

Card Number

Issue No (Switch only)   Valid from (Amex/Switch)

Expires   Signature

Name Mr/Mrs/Ms . . . .
Address . . . .
. . . .
. . . .
. . . . Postcode . . . .
Daytime Tel No . . . .
Email . . . .

Valid to 31/12/05

Free Print – see overleaf

Would you like to find out more about Francis Frith?

We have recently recruited some entertaining speakers who are happy to visit local groups, clubs and societies to give an illustrated talk documenting Frith's travels and photographs. If you are a member of such a group and are interested in hosting a presentation, we would love to hear from you.

Our speakers bring with them a small selection of our local town and county books, together with sample prints. They are happy to take orders. A small proportion of the order value is donated to the group who have hosted the presentation. The talks are therefore an excellent way of fundraising for small groups and societies.

Can you help us with information about any of the Frith photographs in this book?

We are gradually compiling an historical record for each of the photographs in the Frith archive. It is always fascinating to find out the names of the people shown in the pictures, as well as insights into the shops, buildings and other features depicted.

If you recognize anyone in the photographs in this book, or if you have information not already included in the author's caption, do let us know. We would love to hear from you, and will try to publish it in future books or articles.

Our production team

Frith books are produced by a small dedicated team at offices in the converted Grade II listed 18th-century barn at Teffont near Salisbury, illustrated above. Most have worked with the Frith Collection for many years. All have in common one quality: they have a passion for the Frith Collection. The team is constantly expanding, but currently includes:

Jason Buck, John Buck, Ruth Butler, Heather Crisp, David Davies, Isobel Hall, Julian Hight, Peter Horne, James Kinnear, Karen Kinnear, Tina Leary, Stuart Login, Amanda Lowe, David Marsh, Sue Molloy, Kate Rotondetto, Dean Scource, Eliza Sackett, Terence Sackett, Sandra Sampson, Adrian Sanders, Sandra Sanger, Julia Skinner, Claire Tarrier, Lewis Taylor, Shelley Tolcher and Lorraine Tuck.